insects &
spiders

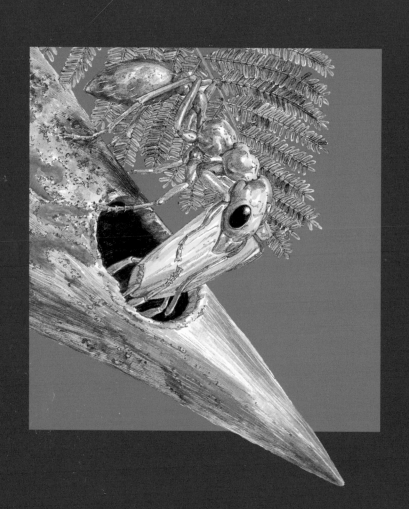

SERIES EDITOR   DAVID SALARIYA
BOOK EDITOR   APRIL McCROSKIE
CONSULTANT   DR. GERALD LEGG

Published in 1995
by Franklin Watts
95 Madison Avenue
New York, NY 10016

Library of Congress Cataloging-in-Publication Data
Clarke, Penny.
 Insects and spiders / by Penny Clarke : illustrated by Carolyn Scrace.
 p. cm. – (Worldwise)
 Includes index.
 Summary: Describes the physical characteristics, lifestyles, and
environmental effects of such insects as ants, beetles, flies, and spiders.
 ISBN 0-531-14365-1 (lib. bdg.) ISBN 0-531-15282-0 (pbk.)
 1. Insects – Juvenile literature. 2. Spiders – Juvenile literature.
 [1. Insects. 2. Spiders.] I. Scrace. Carolyn. ill. II. Title. III. Series.
 QL 467.2 C635 1995   95 – 23323
 595.7 – dc20   CIP
          AC

Printed in Belgium

worldwise
insects &
spiders

Written by
PENNY CLARKE

Illustrated by
CAROLYN SCRACE

Series Created & Designed by
DAVID SALARIYA

FRANKLIN WATTS
A Division of Scholastic Inc.
New York • London • Hong Kong
Sydney • Danbury, Connecticut

CONTENTS

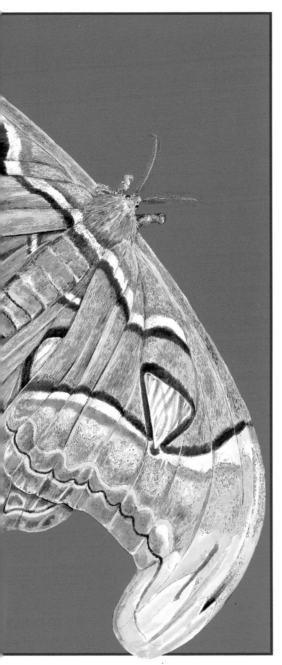

Insects and spiders

first appeared on Earth over 350 million years ago. In contrast, humans appeared only 2.5 million years ago. Today there are over a million known living species of insect and more are discovered each year. Spiders appeared around the same time as insects. Insects are food for spiders. But insects also help feed us. In fact, some insects are essential to human life. Insects carry pollen from plant to plant. This is called pollination, and without it, plants cannot grow seeds and fruit for us to eat.

There are 20,000 different kinds of wasp. Hornets are the largest. The three different parts of the hornet's body are very easy to see.

Insects come in a huge variety of shapes, sizes, and colors, but they all have one thing in common – their bodies are divided into three parts. These are the head, the thorax, (the middle part), and the abdomen, the largest part. All insects also have three pairs of legs. If you see a small creature and think it might be an insect, check its body. If you can see three parts, it is an insect.

Hornets have two pairs of transparent wings.

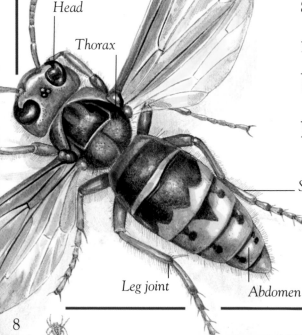

Antenna

Head

Thorax

Sense hairs on legs

All insects have three pairs of legs. Flying insects have one or two pairs of wings.

Leg joint

Abdomen

Brightly colored body is a warning to other animals.

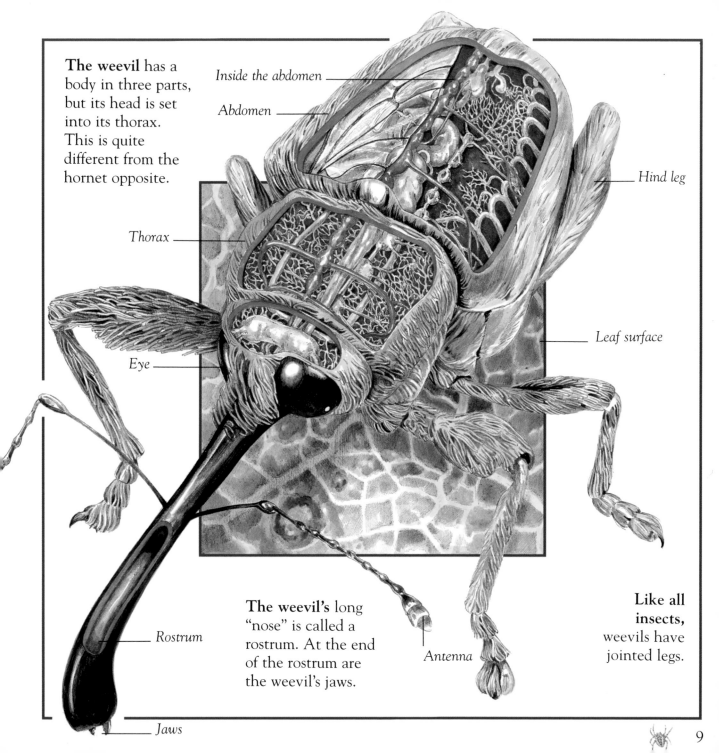

The weevil has a body in three parts, but its head is set into its thorax. This is quite different from the hornet opposite.

Inside the abdomen

Abdomen

Hind leg

Thorax

Leaf surface

Eye

The weevil's long "nose" is called a rostrum. At the end of the rostrum are the weevil's jaws.

Antenna

Like all insects, weevils have jointed legs.

Rostrum

Jaws

9

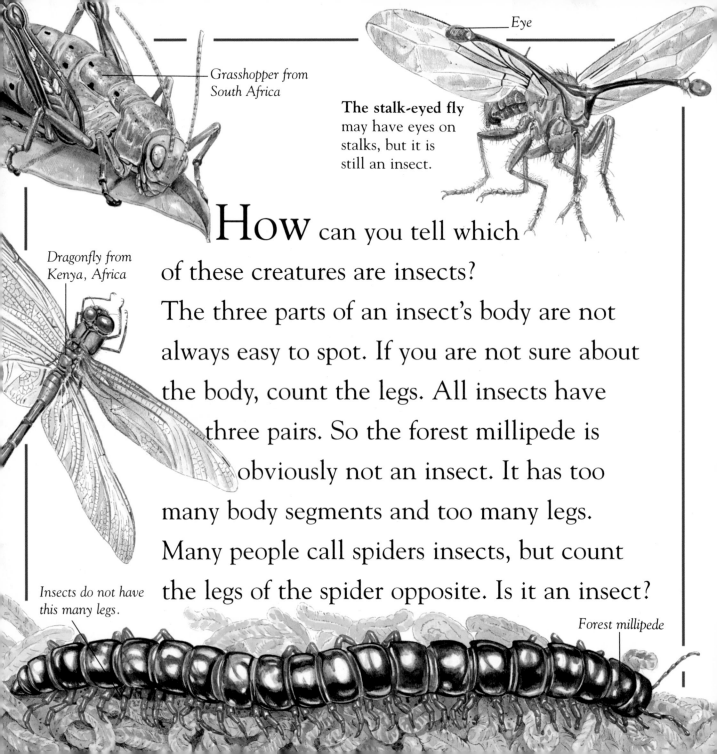

Grasshopper from
South Africa

Eye

The stalk-eyed fly
may have eyes on
stalks, but it is
still an insect.

Dragonfly from
Kenya, Africa

How can you tell which
of these creatures are insects?
The three parts of an insect's body are not
always easy to spot. If you are not sure about
the body, count the legs. All insects have
three pairs. So the forest millipede is
obviously not an insect. It has too
many body segments and too many legs.
Many people call spiders insects, but count
the legs of the spider opposite. Is it an insect?

Insects do not have
this many legs.

Forest millipede

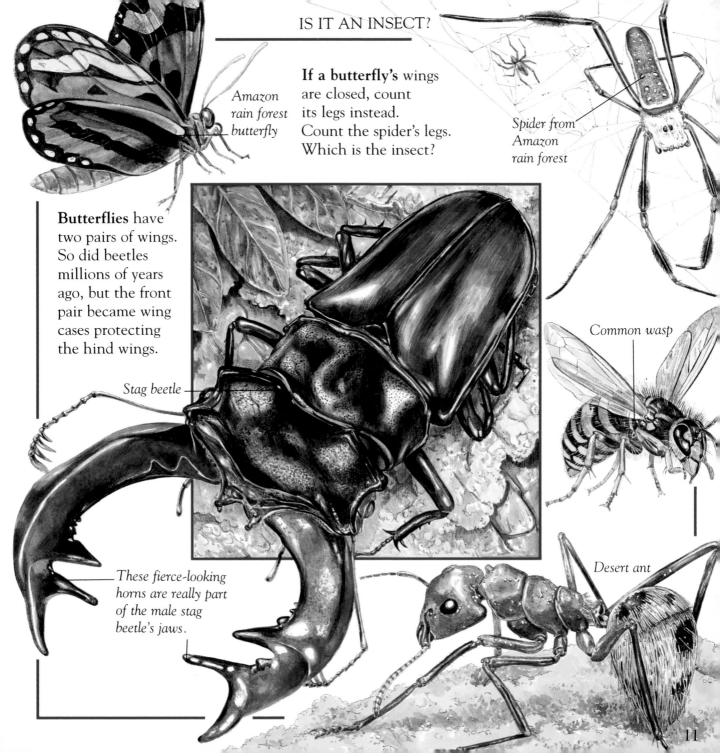

If a butterfly's wings are closed, count its legs instead. Count the spider's legs. Which is the insect?

Amazon rain forest butterfly

Spider from Amazon rain forest

Butterflies have two pairs of wings. So did beetles millions of years ago, but the front pair became wing cases protecting the hind wings.

Stag beetle

Common wasp

These fierce-looking horns are really part of the male stag beetle's jaws.

Desert ant

11

Most insects fly. Their

wings grow from the thorax, the middle part of the body. Each wing is made from two very thin membranes. Some insects, like flies and bees, have transparent wings. Others, like butterflies and moths, have wings covered with tiny, colored scales. The wings are stiffened by a network of veins. These are the dark lines you see in a fly's wings.

Bumblebees are strong fliers, although they do not have a streamlined shape like a bird or a jet plane. On the back leg is the pollen basket, a mass of pollen the bee has collected.

The locust has two pairs of wings. Other insects, like flies (page 27) and beetles (page 11), have only one pair.

Muscles in the thorax move the insect's wings up and down.

Muscles at the base of the wings help the insect change direction.

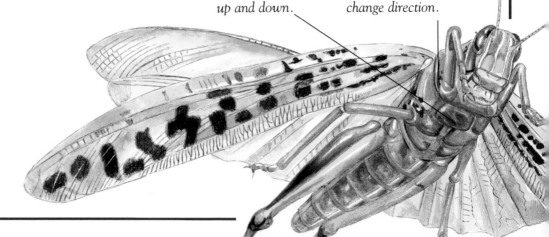

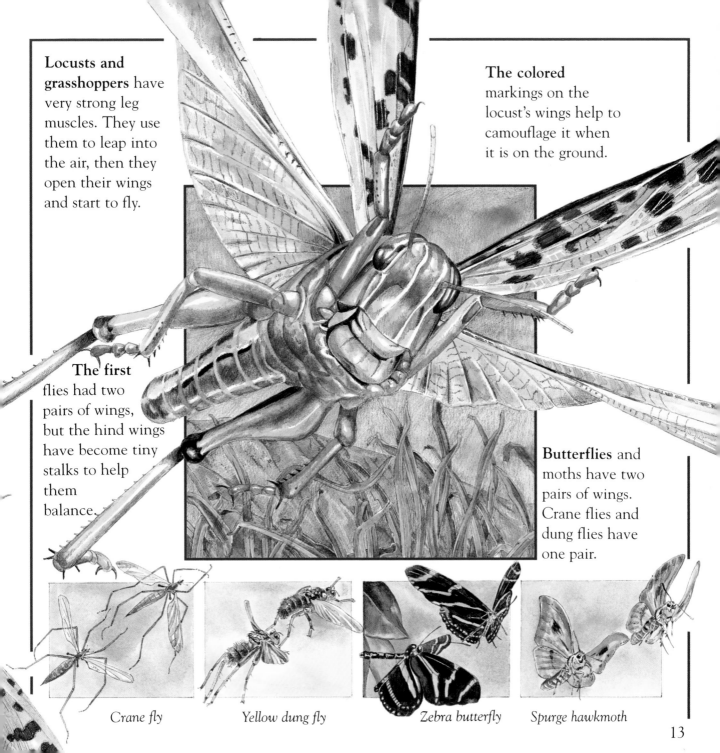

Locusts and grasshoppers have very strong leg muscles. They use them to leap into the air, then they open their wings and start to fly.

The colored markings on the locust's wings help to camouflage it when it is on the ground.

The first flies had two pairs of wings, but the hind wings have become tiny stalks to help them balance.

Butterflies and moths have two pairs of wings. Crane flies and dung flies have one pair.

Crane fly

Yellow dung fly

Zebra butterfly

Spurge hawkmoth

13

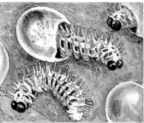

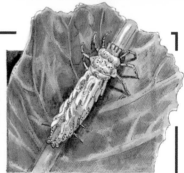

The eggs hatch into caterpillars. They eat the egg cases, and then the leaves. Caterpillars are the larvae of butterflies and moths.

When the caterpillar has stored enough energy, it fastens itself to a twig and changes into a pupa. Inside the pupa's case the adult develops.

A moth lays her eggs on the food the caterpillars will eat when they hatch. The caterpillar does not look like the adult. It has to change into a chrysalis or pupa before it does. This change is called metamorphosis. Some insects, like grasshoppers, look like tiny adults when they hatch. Because they do not change so much, scientists say they have incomplete metamorphosis.

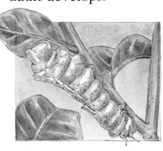
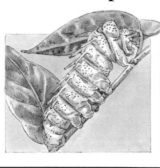
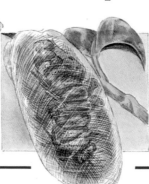

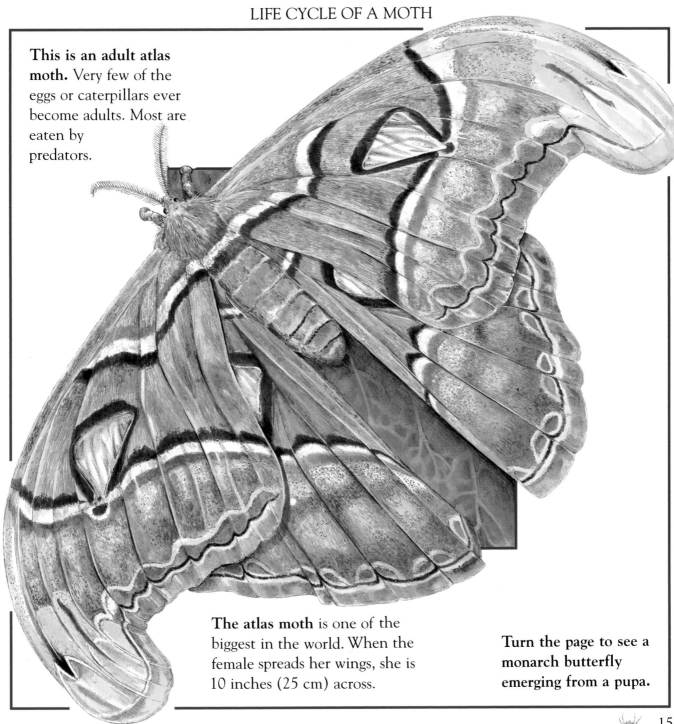

This is an adult atlas moth. Very few of the eggs or caterpillars ever become adults. Most are eaten by predators.

The atlas moth is one of the biggest in the world. When the female spreads her wings, she is 10 inches (25 cm) across.

Turn the page to see a monarch butterfly emerging from a pupa.

15

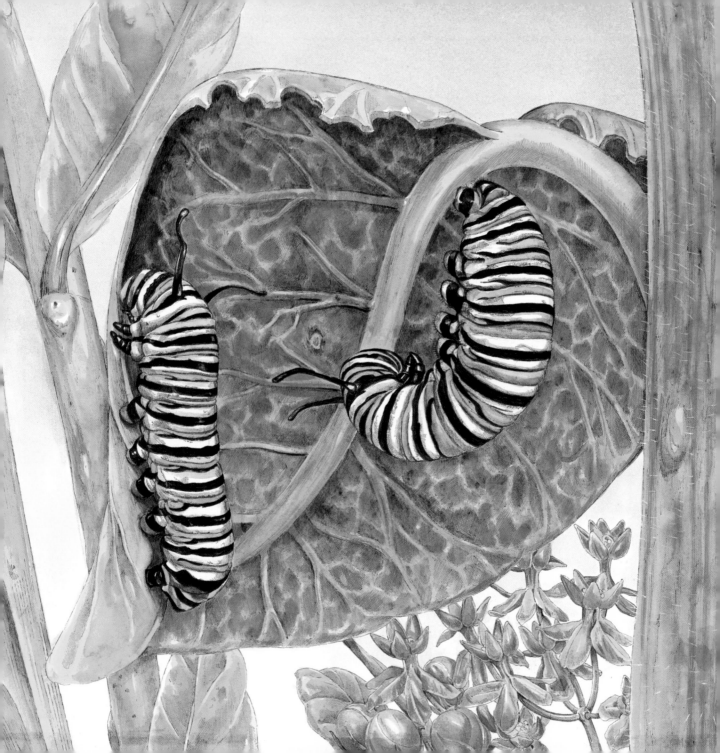

The female garden spider makes a sheet of silk to lay her eggs on.

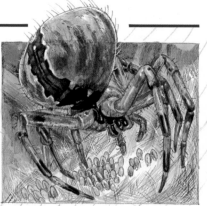

She lays hundreds of eggs on the sheet before wrapping them in a ball of silk.

Then she fixes the ball under a leaf. Female wolf spiders carry the ball around with them.

When spiderlings (young spiders)

hatch from their eggs, they look like miniature adults. Like insects, spiders do not have a skeleton inside their bodies as we do. Instead, they have a rigid outer case, the exoskeleton. To grow, the spiderlings have to shed (molt) their outer case at regular intervals and grow a new, bigger one. Although all spiderlings grow, some have to grow more than others. This is because the females of most species of spider are larger than the males.

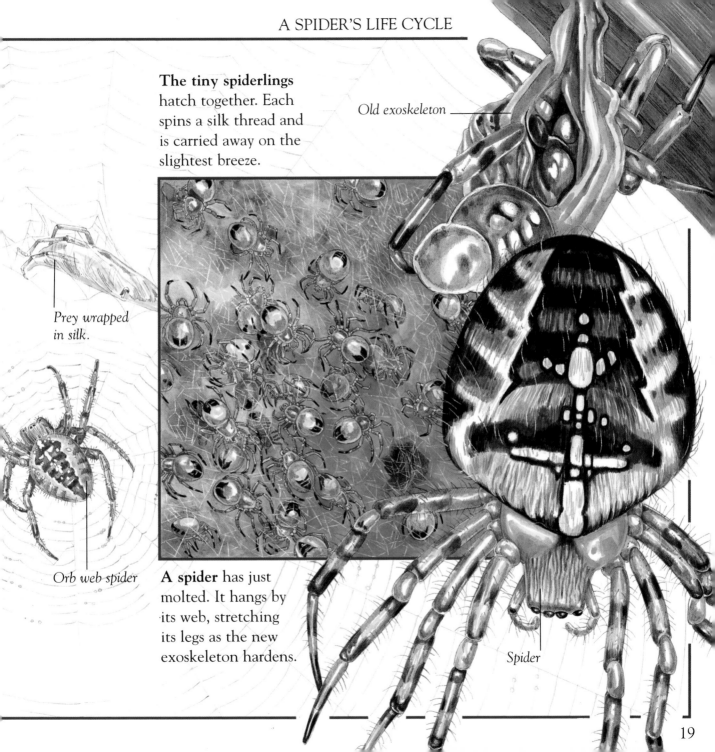

The tiny spiderlings hatch together. Each spins a silk thread and is carried away on the slightest breeze.

Old exoskeleton

Prey wrapped in silk.

Orb web spider

A spider has just molted. It hangs by its web, stretching its legs as the new exoskeleton hardens.

Spider

19

Most spiders eat insects, though a few big tropical ones eat hummingbirds. Spiders catch their food in many different ways. Some stalk it. Others are camouflaged and wait, almost invisible, until their prey passes. Then they lunge forward to grab it. Others trap food in webs made from silk. Spiders cannot bite or chew. So they inject digestive juices into the prey. These turn the insect's body into liquid that the spider can then suck up.

A trapdoor spider lays down threads from its lair. If an insect trips on one, the spider leaps out to catch it.

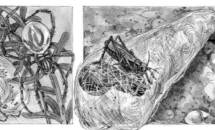

Water spiders trap prey in an underwater web.

Purse web spiders kill prey through the silk "purse."

This jumping spider eats the young of other jumping spiders.

A tarantula waits by its hole for passing prey.

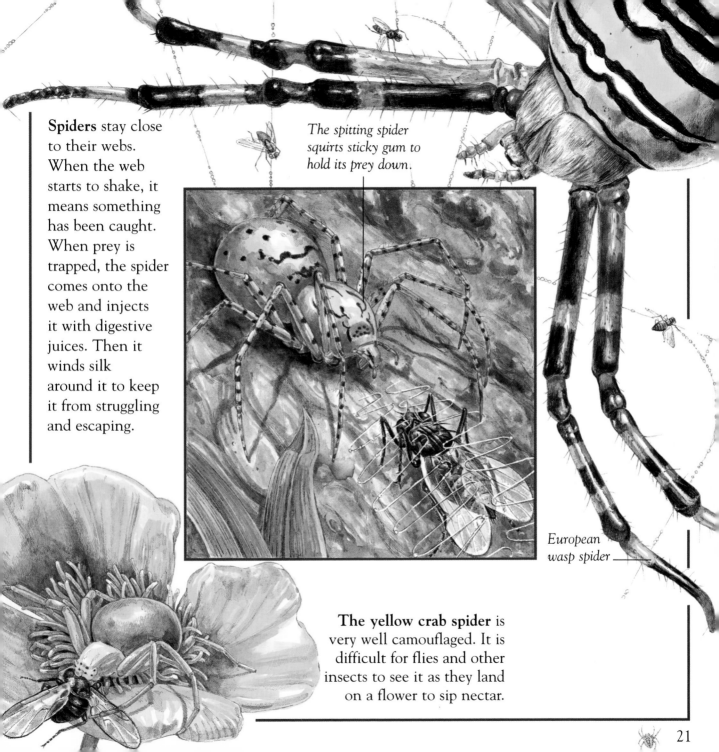

Spiders stay close to their webs. When the web starts to shake, it means something has been caught. When prey is trapped, the spider comes onto the web and injects it with digestive juices. Then it winds silk around it to keep it from struggling and escaping.

The spitting spider squirts sticky gum to hold its prey down.

European wasp spider

The yellow crab spider is very well camouflaged. It is difficult for flies and other insects to see it as they land on a flower to sip nectar.

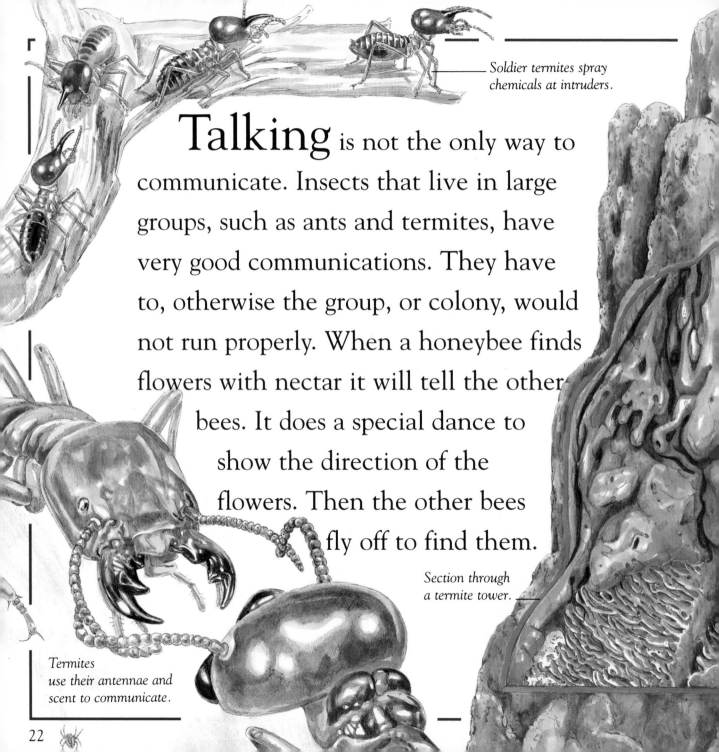

Soldier termites spray
chemicals at intruders.

Talking is not the only way to communicate. Insects that live in large groups, such as ants and termites, have very good communications. They have to, otherwise the group, or colony, would not run properly. When a honeybee finds flowers with nectar it will tell the other bees. It does a special dance to show the direction of the flowers. Then the other bees fly off to find them.

Section through
a termite tower.

Termites
use their antennae and
scent to communicate.

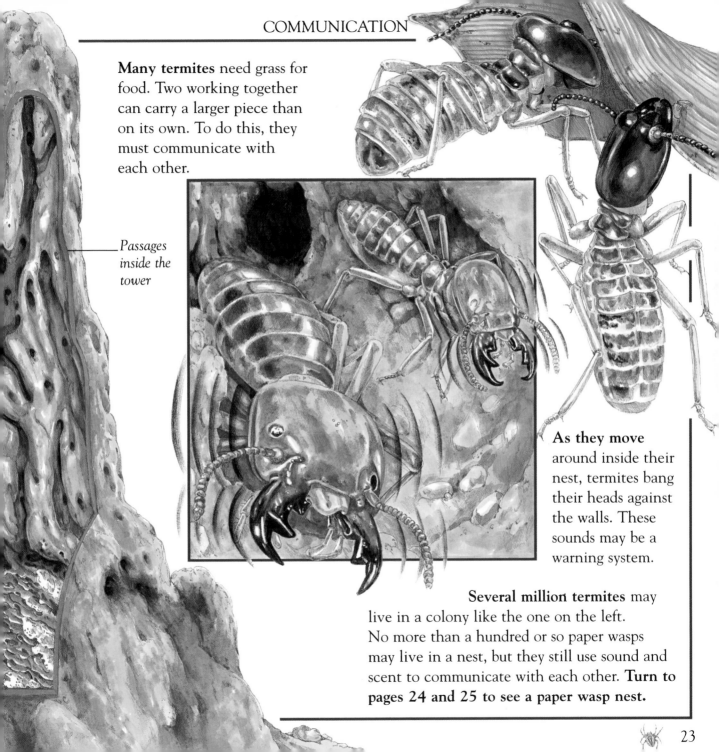

Many termites need grass for food. Two working together can carry a larger piece than on its own. To do this, they must communicate with each other.

Passages inside the tower

As they move around inside their nest, termites bang their heads against the walls. These sounds may be a warning system.

Several million termites may live in a colony like the one on the left. No more than a hundred or so paper wasps may live in a nest, but they still use sound and scent to communicate with each other. **Turn to pages 24 and 25 to see a paper wasp nest.**

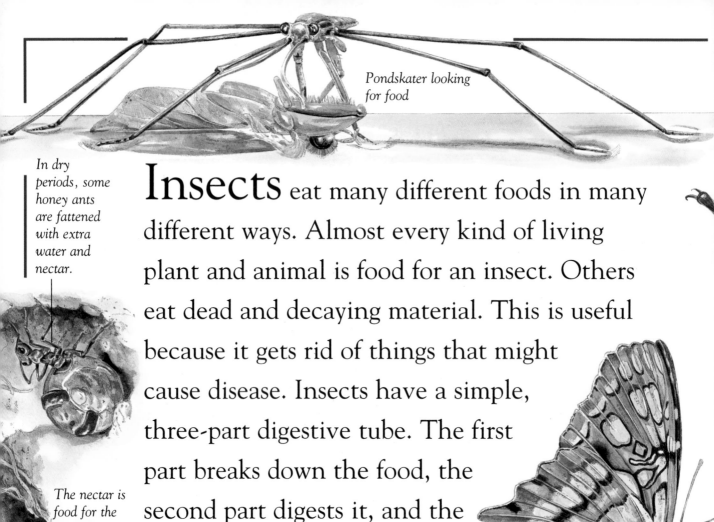

Pondskater looking for food

In dry periods, some honey ants are fattened with extra water and nectar.

The nectar is food for the rest of the colony.

Insects eat many different foods in many different ways. Almost every kind of living plant and animal is food for an insect. Others eat dead and decaying material. This is useful because it gets rid of things that might cause disease. Insects have a simple, three-part digestive tube. The first part breaks down the food, the second part digests it, and the third part excretes anything the insect cannot digest.

A dung-eating butterfly that lives in the southern U.S.A.

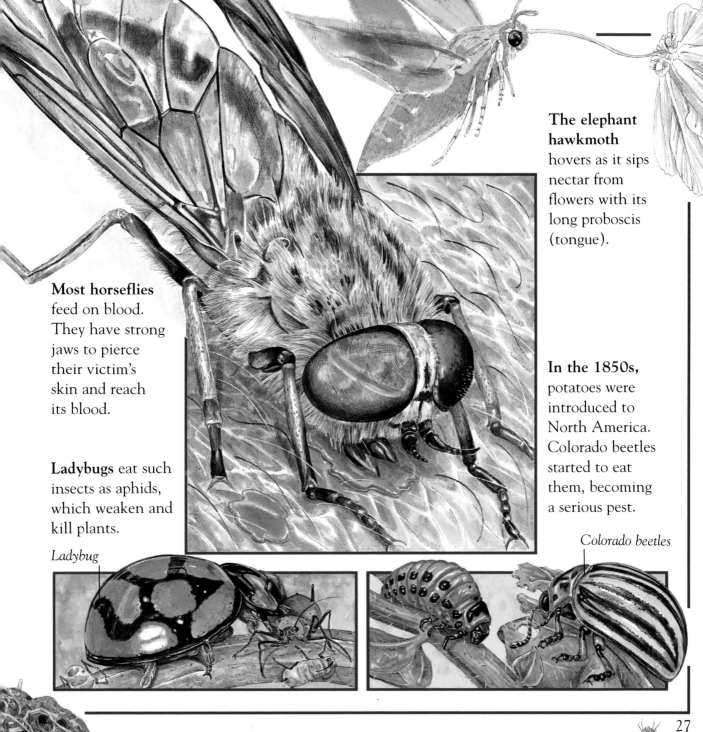

The elephant hawkmoth hovers as it sips nectar from flowers with its long proboscis (tongue).

Most horseflies feed on blood. They have strong jaws to pierce their victim's skin and reach its blood.

Ladybugs eat such insects as aphids, which weaken and kill plants.

Ladybug

In the 1850s, potatoes were introduced to North America. Colorado beetles started to eat them, becoming a serious pest.

Colorado beetles

27

After two or three years living in water, the dragonfly nymph climbs up the stem of a water plant. Soon its skin splits and the adult dragonfly comes out. It stays motionless while its wings and body harden; then it flies away.

Pondskaters skim over the water's surface, hunting drowning insects.

Ponds, streams, and rivers are homes to many different insects.

Some, like the great diving beetle, spend all their lives in water. Others, like dragonflies, live in water when they are young, only leaving it to become adults. Some spiders live in water, too. Instead of a web, they spin a "diving bell" to trap oxygen so they can breathe underwater.

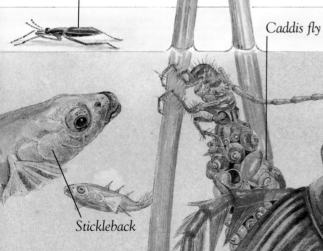

Caddis fly

Great diving beetle

Dragonfly larvae

Stickleback

28

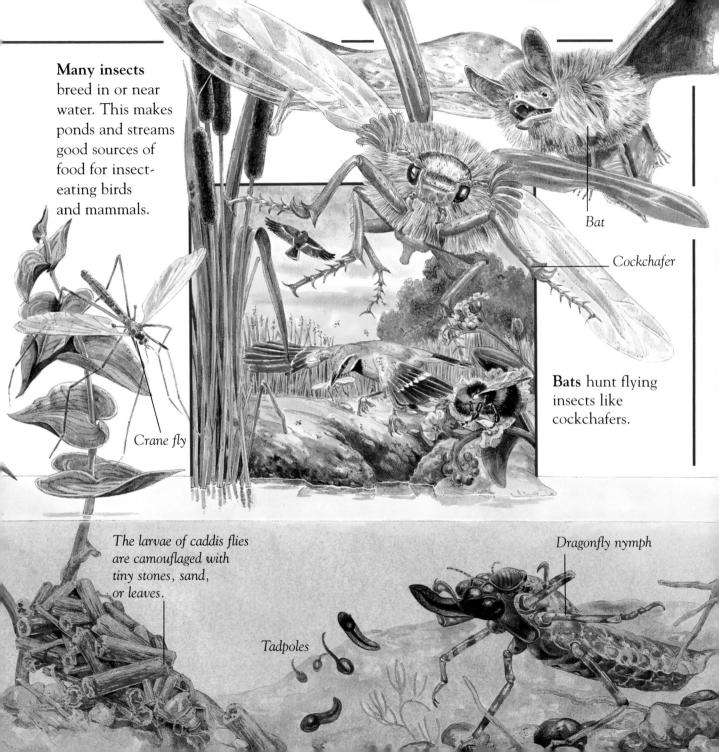

Many insects breed in or near water. This makes ponds and streams good sources of food for insect-eating birds and mammals.

Crane fly

Bat

Cockchafer

Bats hunt flying insects like cockchafers.

The larvae of caddis flies are camouflaged with tiny stones, sand, or leaves.

Tadpoles

Dragonfly nymph

Woodlands in areas

Bumblebee

Musk beetle

Burnet moth

Ladybug

Caterpillars of tortoiseshell butterfly

with a temperate climate are full of insects. Some live in the treetops, others in the small cracks of tree bark. And many live among the fallen leaves on the ground. Butterflies flit across sunny tracks, but avoid the denser woodland. Bees like the fields and meadows, because that is where most flowers grow.

Insects break up the leaves, eat them, and scurry about among them, allowing air in to help them rot. Without insects, it would take years for the leaves to rot. Rotted leaves form leaf mold, which helps the trees and plants grow strongly. Without leaf mold, the trees would soon take all the nutrients from the soil and become weak.

Wolf spiders do not catch their prey in webs. Instead, they stalk an insect before pouncing on it.

Burying beetle

In spring, parent birds collect the caterpillars of butterflies and moths to feed their young.

Common wasp

Hover fly

Rhinoceros beetle

Wolf spider

Wood ant

The trees in rain forests grow very tall and close together. Climbing plants with thick stems loop around the trees. Little light reaches the ground, so most rain forest creatures live high up in the canopy, where there is plenty of light. Brilliantly colored birds and butterflies flash among the leaves. Tiny hummingbirds may be trapped by bird-eating spiders. On the ground, army ants eat any living thing that is in their way.

Leafcutter ant

Leafcutter ants live on fungi. They grow it in their nests on pieces of leaves they cut from nearby plants.

Tree hopper

This plant is not full of thorns, just tree hoppers that look like thorns.

Army ants move in a column – just like an army on the march.

Army ants

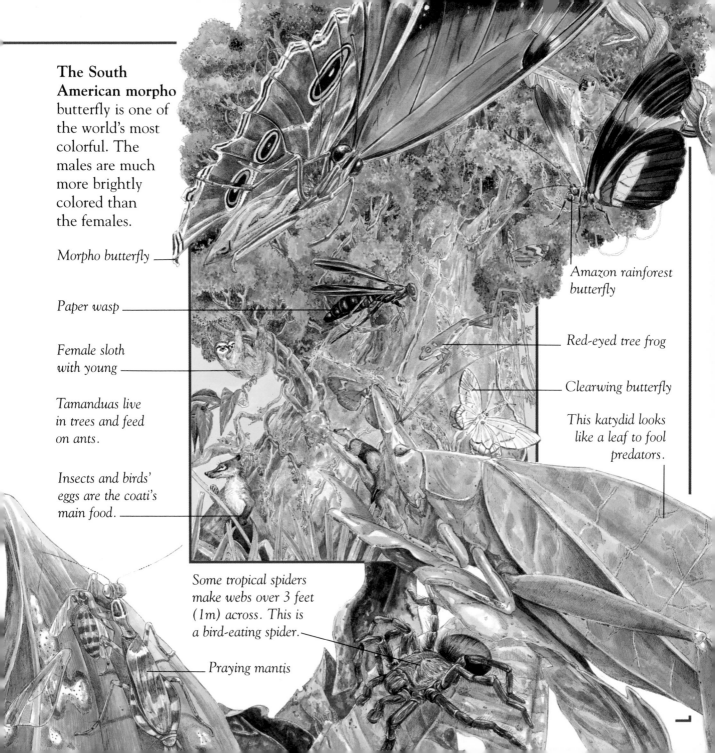

The South American morpho butterfly is one of the world's most colorful. The males are much more brightly colored than the females.

Morpho butterfly

Paper wasp

Female sloth with young

Tamanduas live in trees and feed on ants.

Insects and birds' eggs are the coati's main food.

Amazon rainforest butterfly

Red-eyed tree frog

Clearwing butterfly

This katydid looks like a leaf to fool predators.

Some tropical spiders make webs over 3 feet (1m) across. This is a bird-eating spider.

Praying mantis

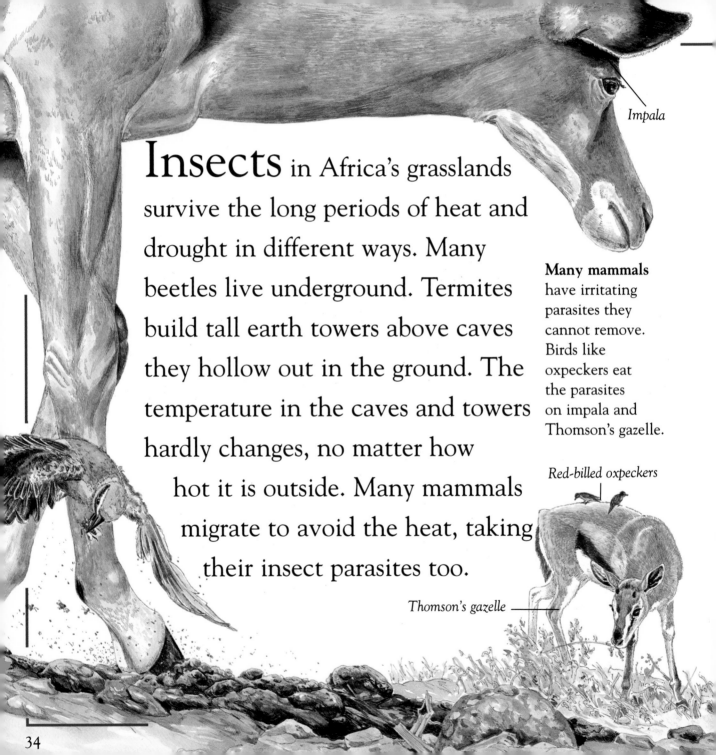

Impala

Insects in Africa's grasslands survive the long periods of heat and drought in different ways. Many beetles live underground. Termites build tall earth towers above caves they hollow out in the ground. The temperature in the caves and towers hardly changes, no matter how hot it is outside. Many mammals migrate to avoid the heat, taking their insect parasites too.

Many mammals have irritating parasites they cannot remove. Birds like oxpeckers eat the parasites on impala and Thomson's gazelle.

Red-billed oxpeckers

Thomson's gazelle

Acacia thorn ants live in the strong thorns of acacia trees. The trees' leaf buds are food for their young, so the ants are not out in the heat for long.

Acacia thorn ant

Termites build their towers from tiny pellets of earth which they cement together with saliva. Several million termites may live in the caves below.

The aardvark eats termites. It breaks into the nests with its strong claws and scoops up the termites with its 18-inch (45-cm)-long tongue.

Aardvark

Termite tower

Dung beetles

Dung beetles gather up dung, roll it into a ball, and take it into their burrows. There they can feed in safety away from the heat.

A species dies out if not enough adults survive to mate and produce young. Insects have many defense tactics to help ensure they survive. Butterflies may imitate leaves, and tree hoppers look like thorns to fool enemies. Wasps have bright colors to make predators think they are poisonous. Ants squirt acid at attackers. Large spots make harmless caterpillars and butterflies look fierce.

Stick insects look like sticks.

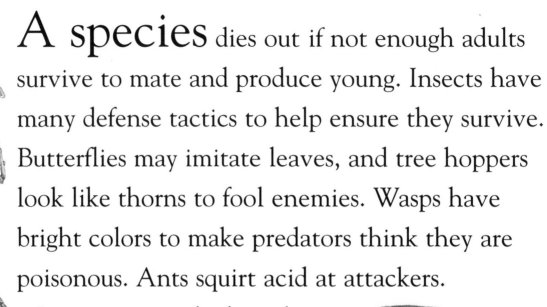

One moment an attacker sees a caterpillar, the next a large angry-looking creature with huge "eyes."

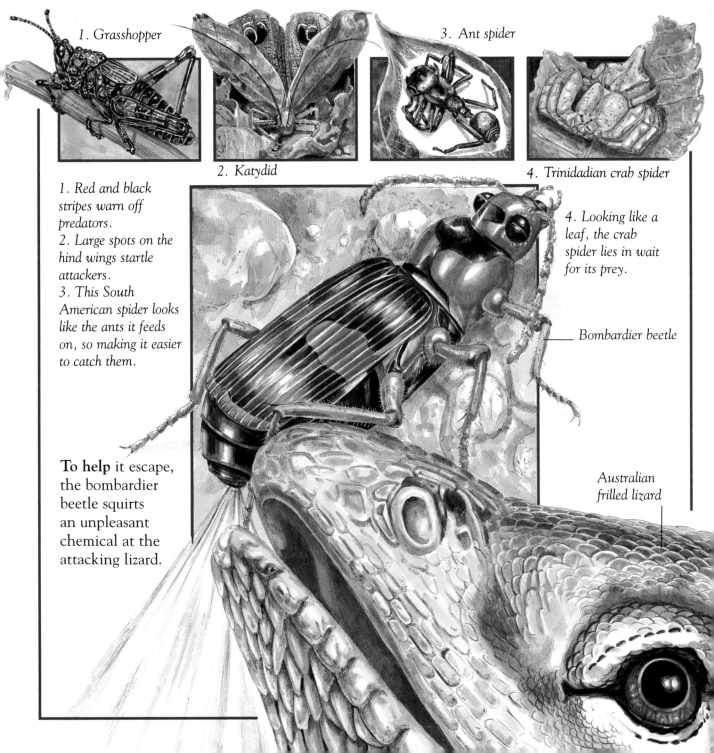

1. Grasshopper

2. Katydid

3. Ant spider

4. Trinidadian crab spider

1. Red and black stripes warn off predators.

2. Large spots on the hind wings startle attackers.

3. This South American spider looks like the ants it feeds on, so making it easier to catch them.

4. Looking like a leaf, the crab spider lies in wait for its prey.

Bombardier beetle

To help it escape, the bombardier beetle squirts an unpleasant chemical at the attacking lizard.

Australian frilled lizard

USEFUL WORDS

Abdomen Rear, and largest, part of an insect's body.

Antenna (plural **antennae**) Insects have two on their heads and use them for feeling, touching, and communicating.

Camouflage Markings on a creature that allow it to blend in with its surroundings.

Chrysalis Pupa of a butterfly or moth.

Incomplete metamorphosis Life cycle of insects when the young always look very like the adults they will grow into.

Larva (plural **larvae**) Stage in an insect's life between leaving the egg and becoming a pupa.

Mammal Animal which is fed on its mother's milk when it is young.

Membrane Very thin skinlike structure.

Metamorphosis Life cycle of insects in which there is complete change in shape and appearance.

Migrate Move from one area to another according to the time of year.

Nectar Sweet fluid produced by flowers.

Parasite Something that lives and feeds on another living creature.

Predator Creature that hunts for prey.

Prey Creature that is hunted as food.

Pupa (plural **pupae**) Stage in many insects' lives between larva and adult.

Species Group of animals or plants that look alike, live in the same way, and produce young that do the same.

Temperate Climate that is not very hot, very dry, very cold, or very wet.

Thorax Middle of the three parts of an insect's body.

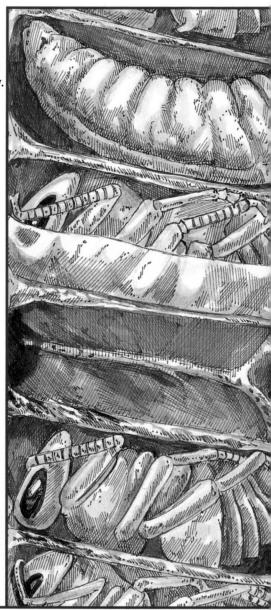

INDEX

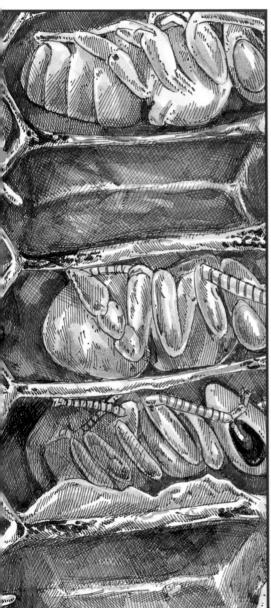